Be

Strong

Enough

Judy Prescott Marshall

Judy Prescott Marshall

BE STRONG ENOUGH

JUDY PRESCOTT MARSHALL

Judy Prescott Marshall

ISBN 978-0-9910273-0-9 (soft cover)

ISBN 978-0-9910273-1-6 (e-book)

Second edition. 11/01/2020

For my Saving Grace

Dear Friends,

This book is for anyone with big dreams. The message is simple. Believe in yourself, walk with integrity, work hard, and trust in God. Your life may not turn out exactly the way you had hoped or expected but it will be so much better than you could have ever imagined. If...you believe.

I was at a crossroad and I had no idea how I was supposed to support myself. I sat down on my chase lounge, bowed my head and asked the Lord for a number and this is what He gave to me. 45 I opened my Bible turned to Psalms 45:1 and read: "My heart is indicting a good matter: I speak of the things which I have made touching the king: my tongue is the pen of a ready writer." Can you imagine how I felt reading – a ready writer?!

From that moment on, I did not let my education or the lack of one stop me from pursuing my dream of becoming a paid writer.

Every day, I practiced my profession. I read daily. Made sure I wrote a minimum of 1000 words and I took care of myself physically. Most of all I never listened to the naysayers in my head.

Xoxo,

Judy.

Be strong enough. Seriously! Be the person you want to be. Be strong enough to take risks. The rules are simple: Dream. Believe and Achieve. With a GED in one hand and a fist full of ambition, I made this book for my BFF ~ (book friend forever) You! My wish for you is to live your best life at any age. Make every day triumphant.

Be Strong Enough Motto ~ We have this hope as an anchor for the soul, firm and secure. Hebrews 6:19

Teresa loves tag sales, flea markets and thrift stores. She could take an old table and make it new again. From whitewashing to reupholstering to tearing furniture apart and turning it into something brand new. What used to be an old dresser now serves as a coffee bar. She turned her passion into a lucrative business. And so can you.

Believe in yourself! Be brave when fear is behind you. Be courageous in all that you do. Hell, be adventurous. Do something wonderful for yourself. Be happy every day. Be healthy for you. Most of all…believe in YOU!

I'm trying to create a beautiful ripple effect called inspiration. You can help me by inspiring someone in your life. A relative, friend, or a neighbor.

I know you have an idea. You have a tremendous amount of passion. It's time you start sharing your ideas with the world. Start with a conversation. Talk to someone who believes in you. Or do what I did. Dive right in. Begin with a blog. www.wordpress.com It's user friendly. Make sure to use hashtags. #bestrongenough #believe

Heidi loved making soap. One day she started blogging on www.tumblr.com about her experiences. Then she started posting her recipes and photos. One year later, a publisher offered her a book deal!

It's Friday night. Time to be naughty. Grab your galentines and enjoy yourselves!

Do you know what a coyote sounds like in the night? How about a barred owl? I invite you to open your window, sit down and listen to the sounds all around you.

I would never go hiking in the dark…not alone anyway. Nor should you.

Be fearless in all that you do. If you're faced with hard times, believe that you are strong enough to get through anything. If you are in need of a financial miracle, buy a stranger a cup of coffee. Be a blessing to others. Wake up every day and look in the mirror. Say, "I am fearless. I'm excited about my future."

I could be naked in a cardboard box and still I would be the happiest woman alive. I walk by faith. Live life…every day! Won't you join me?

Be kind to others. See that person sitting alone. Be the person who sits beside him or her. Pay for someone else's groceries. You will be blessed one-hundred times more. There is always someone else in greater need. Be the one who stands out. Make every day your best!

"You are my hiding place: you will protect me from trouble.

And surround me with songs of deliverance."

~ Psalms 32:7

Keep your body tuned up. A healthy body is a happy body. Okay, painless body. If you are over fifty, yoga is extremely important for your bones, muscles and best of all flexibility. Pilates is a great way to exercise without all the sweat. Aerobics is definitely for the youthful. Seriously! You have to be in shape to tackle that strenuous activity.

I go hiking at sunrise so I can hear the early morning birds'

wake up the ground creatures.

You must have a bucket list. Seriously, grab a pen, paper and start writing. Here's mine: Inspire as many people as I can. Read every day. Write numerous bestselling novels. Garden, hike and kayak whenever possible. Learn to play the saxophone. Visit the Grand Old Opry House. Travel to Italy.

Never give up! The woman standing on the top rung didn't

fall up there.

It is easier to say no to your vendors than it is to tell your bank why your account is overdrawn. Mind your money. Never borrow money when you need it the most. A good business owner assigns the people to the right jobs. You can have the best strategy in the world but it has no value without the right people to execute it.

Good business minded people don't have to have a really high-IQ, but they do have to have a good heart.

Take a class. Perhaps a master writing class. Maybe you have always wanted to learn how to paint, knit or swim. It is never too late to learn something new. You could get your degree. There's something out there for everyone. Be a part of something wonderful.

Before tomorrow arrives, I do the prep work today.

You deserve nice things. A beautiful home. Your home is a reflection of you. Start by cleaning one room at a time. Clean it from top to bottom. Stand back and admire your accomplishments.

Pick a day to clean. Any day, other than the weekend. Weekends are for family, friends and farmer's markets.

Pick Hump day.

Courage is when I'm scared to death but I hold my nose and dive in anyway.

Coloring. It's the new craze. Gather a few friends. Sit down and you will be amazed at how much fun everyone will have. Besides, coloring can be very therapeutic. So let your creativity take over. Set out on a colorful journey.

Start a garden club in your area. Share plants and ideas. Get outdoors!

How many times have you heard, "Communication is the key to every relationship?" Whether it be at home or in the workplace, say what you mean and mean what you say. If something is bothering you, don't carry it around for days on end. Talk about it. Remember, there is healing in open dialogue.

Hiking during the month of May...the air is full of honeysuckle in New York. What does your neighborhood smell like?

Try to cook all your meals. Avoid packaged foods as much as possible. Plan your meals ahead of time. Post a weekly menu right on the fridge. Even if you live alone, it is better to make more and freeze it for another day.

Here's one of my favorite quick and easy healthy snack recipes. Energy bars!

Mix together in a food processor –

4 cups of graham cracker with 1 cup of butter. Then spread onto a 9X13 baking sheet.

Layer the following ingredients, one at a time:

1 ½ cups of semi-sweet chocolate chips.

1 cup of chopped walnuts.

1 cup of shredded coconut.

Drizzle one can (14oz.) of condensed milk on top.

Bake 350 ° for 30 minutes. I don't cut mine until the next day. Cut 24 snack size bars. So good!

Dance when you feel the rhythm deep in your soul. Even if you have to dance alone.

Remember when you were a little girl or boy and you put a buttercup under your chin? Well, I hope that same adventurous child is still in you today.

A diet is only as good as the individual creating the meal plan. My advice is to eat small portions. Remember food is fuel. You have to eat. Try to create a daily meal plan that contains the right amount of protein, carbohydrates, dairy, fruit and vegetables. I eat five small meals a day. I use a salad plate for all of my meals.

Drink water, herbal teas, seltzer, and club soda. Incorporate foods such as nuts, spices, whole grain *not* whole wheat. Eat a teaspoon of peanut butter to stop sugar cravings. And remember…never eat two hours before bedtime.

Write a garden journal. Document all changes and transplants. You'll be happy you did.

Live the life that you dream about. Share your accomplishments. I was fourteen when I wrote my first story. A Christmas story. By seventeen, I was attending the prestigious Upward Bound Program – the program Oprah Winfrey won the leadership award *and* four years later, I was honored to win the same award.

2018 ~ I wrote *Still Crazy*, publication date April 1, 2021.

2019, I wrote *Be Strong Enough* for my book club friends.

2020, I am editing *The Inn in Rhode Island* to be released April 1, 2022.

At night when I close my eyes, I see my name on

The New York Time's Best Seller's List.

I am not afraid to dream with my eyes wide open. I believe when your heart and mind are on the same page…no one can stop you. Now turn your dreams into your new plan.

Never stop dreaming!

You are the chocolate in my chip! #BFF

Eat from the bounty of a garden. If you can't grow your own fruit and vegetables, there are several ways to buy fresh produce. Farmers' markets are popping up everywhere these days. Grocery stores are stocking up with locally grown produce and organic items. Feast on more of the good stuff and you won't crave the junk food. I promise!

Forever the fox in my hole! Meaning…book friends are like soldiers – they'll always have your back.

When it comes to education. Learn from experience, mentors, and good business-minded people.

When the wind doesn't blow my way, I put on my lipstick and thank God for my next opportunity.

Exercise every day. Start by walking fifteen minutes, turn around and BOOM…you are on your way to a healthier you. It is vital that you remember to breathe properly. Try this simple exercise. Sitting or standing, stretch your arms out to your sides. As you raise them high above your head, breathe in through your nose. When you lower your arms, exhale as if you're blowing out a candle.

You just told your lungs to send your head some oxygen.

Life was tough for me but I was so much stronger...

Have hope and forgiveness in your heart. Lead by example. Be the person others can look up to. Family is everything. Often, a family member is someone you did not grow up with. You never know whose name will be written in your life book.

Take photos of your gardens.

Forgiveness is the most essential ingredient we can bestow upon ourselves in our lives. It allows us to let go of hardships and make a fresh start. Open your mind. Allow compassion to increase. Now and in the future. You have to forgive in order to move forward. You must believe that faith and love will guide you.

Learn to forgive. Your heart, mind and soul will thank you.

Even better than family are the friends we get to hand select to be in our lives. A good friend is always there for you. As you are for her. Or him. A friend will listen. Cry with you. Never judge you. There is no greater gift than that of a good friend. A strong friendship is worth more than all the gold in the world. So choose wisely. It takes years to build trust and seconds to destroy it.

Gardening 101 Remember the first year – they sleep, second year –they creep and the third – leap.

Judy Prescott Marshall

When you see a beautiful garden. It's okay to admire the first flower that you see. Just make sure to pick the best flower in the garden.

When your heart is open and your mind is set on finding true love.

Remember the rules of the garden.

My favorite all vegetable soup for slimming down.

Large soup pot.

¼ cup of olive oil

1 head of any color cabbage – chopped.

2 cloves of garlic – chopped.

2 cups of water.

2 cans (14 oz.) stewed tomatoes – chopped.

Any or all of the following:

1 onion – chopped.

1 cup of fresh green beans – chopped.

1 cup of chopped spinach.

1 cup of kale – chopped.

1 cup of fresh or frozen peas.

Cook 30 minutes. Enjoy! Psst, you're welcome!

Grieve for as long as you would expect others to grieve for you.

Gabrielle loved to bake. Her homemade chocolates are amazing, and her pies are so picture perfect you hate slicing into them. From cookies to jams and caramels. Gabrielle took her passion for baking to farmers markets all over Maine. #Cha Ching!

Whenever I feel tired, I turn to aromatherapy. I hang sprigs of mint in my shower.

Deborah is a spiritual healer. She believes in love, light and forgiveness. Folks turn to her for uplifting advice. She makes enough money to take care of herself and her loving cat.

Be an inspiration to everyone you meet. It's not hard to inspire. All you have to do is be kind, loving and forgiving.

Snack on frozen peas. They're high in protein.

There is a young child aspiring to be just like you. Mentoring can be very rewarding. There are so many good programs out there. The AWANA program at your local church. Girl and Boy Scouts of America. Summer camp for boys and girls. Be a part of something big.

I use Ban ® roll-on deodorant to STOP the itch from bug
bites.

Every now and then, you need to allow your face to be kissed by the sun. The sun is God's way of providing us with enough UV light that is essential for our bodies to produce vitamin D. Which helps strengthen bones, muscles and the body's immune system. Overexposure to the sun can be damaging. Luckily for you, you only need a few minutes a day. So go ahead and blow kisses to the sky.

My best salad recipe…ever!

Arugula 2 cups chopped.

Pine nuts. ½ cup.

Warm olive oil with sea salt and pepper drizzled on top.

Fresh parmesan cheese.

Thin slices of smoked salmon on the side and 2 pieces of baguette bread spread with goat cheese. #Heaven sent!

Love with all your heart. Keep your heart open. Always love yourself the way you love everyone else. You are special. I know. Because God told me.

When planting bulbs in your garden remember summer bloomers. Allium, Dahlia, and Lily.

To avoid headaches, I do the following: I look up! Notice the top of the trees. Stare at the clouds. Admire how beautiful the mountains connect with each other. Meditate. It's not as hard as you think. Sit quietly or listen to the sound of soothing instruments playing in the background. If you are fortunate to live near a stream, even better. Get outdoors! Start by emptying your mind of all its worries. Visualize a lake on a sunny day. A meadow with wild flowers. Imagine you are the only person for miles. You are happy. You are free from all debt. Life is good. All your dreams are within reach.

Lucille Ball was funny, and she was brave. In today's world…be a Lucille!

Ahh, close your eyes and imagine. Imagine, you are being kissed under the light of the moon. Now feel the magic all around you.

"For I know the plans I have for you."

~ Jeremiah 29:11

From country to classical. Music has a way of lifting our spirits. Touching our hearts. Feeding our souls.

My whole life turned around when I was twelve. Funny? No!

That's when I started counting my blessings.

If you cannot write your strategy or idea on the back of your business card...then it might be too complex to execute. Networking begins by linking all of your contacts in one document. Then by connecting with *their* contacts.

The power of a sneeze. If you sneeze in a room full of people, how many others will be affected? One? Two? And when they sneeze?

That is the power of networking.

"With God all things are possible!"

Matthew 19:26

Rule number one. You must pay yourself. Rule number two. Know your self-worth. Rule number three. Decide to be wealthy. If you truly need every penny you earn in order to survive, then you need to find a way to earn more. In order to pursue my dream of becoming a writer. I ran an ad: *Meticulous housekeeper seeks employment.* A week later, a headhunter from Long Island called and offered me a job. My only request.

They pay me what I was worth. $35.00 per hour.

I planted lavender outside my door – I heard it helps fight Alzheimer. I can only hope. Learning something new every day will definitely help in the fight.

One good deed may turn into numerous acts. And why not?

You have the power to change the world.

Do not judge. You don't know what storm I've asked her to go through.

~ God

If you live alone and you're scared in the night. Put bells on all of your exterior doors. Learn self-defense.

I believe everything happens for a reason and for good reason...I believe!

Play with words and you have a story. Play a game of solitaire. Pick up an instrument and play it for the first time. Play patty cake with a child. Play, play play…every day!

Sail away to an island. Even if you have to close your eyes and imagine.

A good book can take you places. Reading allows us to explore new possibilities. Travel to places far away. Discover new friends. If you're not the reading type, try audio books. They're free at your local library. Join a book club. If you find reading difficult, try reading – large print books with sans serif typeface.

Read every day. I promise you, your mind will thank you.

Understand what drives the other person. What wakes him or her up? What is it they are after in life? You can't fulfill their need until you understand them.

Hard times are expected. Bad times are not so good. Good times are definitely okay.

You decide. Every day you make the decisions. You are the only person in charge of wonderful you. Learn. Grow and move forward.

I was in the seventh grade when a teacher challenged me to write a short story. She recognized a talent within me. Because of her… I wrote my first story. Today, I am thankful to God for blessing me with the ability to share my stories.

Open your eyes to the wonders all around you.

Tecnu ®! It's my secret weapon to poison ivy.

High IQ or God given talent. Which would you rather have?

Believe in yourself. No matter what.

Anyone who has time for drama… is not gardening enough.

Sex releases endorphins. Endorphins reduce pain and make us feel happy. Urinating after sex helps to avoid urinary tract infections.

Marriages are made in heaven. Wait, so is thunder and lightning.

Sing when you are happy. Sing because you don't have the blues.

I no longer have an untold story inside me. How about you?

#BookFriendsForever

Smell everything that is good. Pure. Exciting. The rain. The ocean. Newborn child. Sea salt air. Cookies out of the oven. Fresh cut grass. My favorite – vanilla.

Grab a blanket, book and find yourself a shade tree.

Soul! Not your soul mate. Your inner core. Your immortal essence of a living being. Your principles in life. Your feelings and thoughts.

Your mind has a thought. Your heart feels for...but in the end, your soul reacts!

In my novel, *Still Crazy* – Julie Holliday chose to love all of him. I promise…it's coming to a bookstore near you. Available everywhere books are sold. April 1, 2021!

You need to believe in something. Find your spiritual center. Whatever it is…and don't lose it.

To be a good writer you have to believe in yourself when no one else will.

When was the last time you stood under the stars and gazed?

If you could tell the stars anything…what would you say?

You don't have to be a good writer to write but you do have to write to be good.

If you fail.

Never give up.

Because fail means.

First attempt in learning.

End is not the end.

In fact, end means.

Effort never dies.

If you get no as an answer,

Remember

No means. Next opportunity!

Did you know that a Mulberry tree will not blossom until after the last frost?

Taste everything. Especially life!

Remember why you fell in love.

Try practicing time management for one week. Wake-up. Give thanks. Work out for thirty minutes. Eat. Shower. Work. Even domestic engineers work an eight-hour day. Take a minute to call a family member or friend. Enjoy your favorite beverage. Tea. Right? Most of all take a moment to enjoy time with yourself.

Value every moment and you will have accomplished time management.

Take a walk through a garden. Hike on a safe trail. Borrow a bicycle. Bring a camera. You never know what you'll see. Check out the community calendar in your area. Visit a museum, library, orchard, local farm, iconic landmarks, and historical homes. Google places near you. Start exploring your surroundings. Nowadays, you can travel to a tropical island for less than $500. So what are you waiting for? You deserve a vacation!

I never travel without my heart.

Create your vision board. Take a photo of everything you dream of having, accomplishing, and want. Place the photos where you can see them. Every day, study your photographs. Know in your heart that you can have it all. All you have to do is…believe!

In order to translate your vision into a reality you must take a leadership role.

One word – Mila! Mila was a star before her fifth birthday. She has her own channel and following on YouTube. As of 2019, Mila has over 609,000 subscribers. The moment she started talking about her best friend, Karen aka the nemesis who is always good for a one upper, we were hooked. The world can't get enough of this child prodigy. Mila's "Morning Thought with Mila" has 1,799,970 views. She's funny, chatty, and she's one clever little girl. Together with her twin sister, Emma the girls can add entrepreneurship to their tag line. Thanks to the folks at Target, Mila and Emma have their own fashion line. So go ahead girls tell your stories and please continue to believe in yourselves! #Voice #Creativity

If you're suffering from hair loss or thinning hair, try any one of these ideas:

Soak six fresh sprigs of rosemary in pure vegetable glycerin. Shake every other day for six weeks. Strain into a spray bottle. Use daily by messaging into scalp and brushing. Leave in for one hour. Wash and rinse.

Or, add 20 drops each peppermint, rosemary and lavender essence oil to your daily shampoo. Shake prior to use. Make sure your shampoo does not contain silicones.

Amazing results!

Wake up every day happy. Be thankful for all you have. Be grateful it's a new dawn. A new day. Say, "I am happy. Today, things are going to go great for me."

I wanted to read a story about a strong woman. Therefore, I wrote the book. *Still Crazy* – A strong, loving and passionate wife discovers a handwritten note that has the power to either destroy her or make her stronger yet.

If you added *Still Crazy* to your Goodreads list, thank you.

Figure out how to be paid for doing what you love. Work with people who appreciate you. Work hard because you never know who is watching.

If you fulfill your dream – whatever it may be, you will have done something wonderful in your life.

Is there a story inside you? Start by writing in a journal. Or write an entire novel. It's easy to write a 90,000 word document. It is! In fact, if you write 250 words a day – that's one piece of paper – in one year's time, you will have a complete novel in your hands.

"When the fighter steps into the ring, she knows deep in her heart the moment she looks out into the crowd among her supporters, there are people who wish to see her fall. Win or lose...the fighter will always get back up again."

~ Judy Prescott Marshall

I am dedicated to helping others. 100% of *my* net proceeds from *Be Strong Enough* will go toward assisting women, children and their pets. Everyone should have food on their tables, clothes to wear and a safe place they can call home. Together, we can rebuild lives for women and children in need. Thank you for your support.

Love, Judy.

Photo taken by Judy Prescott Marshall

To learn more contact Judy at

judyprescottmarshall@aol.com

Or visit her website.

https://www.judyprescottmarshall.com

My Saving Grace Lord is you!

Thank you for reading my stories. I welcome your comments. Please post your review on Amazon and GoodReads, it means so much to a writer. I look forward to hearing from you.

My website: www.judyprescottmarshall.com

Visit my blog: www.bestrongenough.com

Follow me:

http://www.twitter.com/01judymarshall

http://www.instagram.com/judyprescottmarshall

http://www.pinterest.com/judyprescottmar/

http://www.facebook.com/judyprescottmarshall

http://www.goodreads.com/user/show/35756418-judy-prescott-marshall

Drop me a line at

judyprescottmarshall@aol.com

Now you have my address...

What's yours?

Fondly, Judy.

#BookFriendsForever

Be Strong Enough